FOREWORD

I0407654

By **Professor Robert Ebo Hinson** (Pro Vice-Chancellor, Ghana Communication Technology University and Council member)

Networking is crucial to the Survival of individuals, institutions, nations, sub-regions blocks and even continents. Networking is the activation of international systematic relationships to foster personal and institutional growth.

This new book on strategic networking is an ideal practitioner guide to developing truthful relationships and deals with topical issues like the transformative power of relationships, international networking and cultural intelligence, building bridges, innovation and adaptability, networking and building relationships in the digital age and overcoming obstacles to networking success.

This is highly recommended reading for individual and institutions looking to attain time professional success.

ACKNOWLEDGEMENT

First and foremost, I extend my deepest gratitude to Almighty God, whose guidance and blessings have been the driving force behind this work. Without His grace, this journey would not have been possible.

To my dear husband, Ruben Opoku-Sarkodie, I owe a debt of heartfelt thanks. Your unwavering support, patience, and constant encouragement have been the foundation of this endeavor. Your love and belief in me have turned my dreams into reality, and for that, I am forever grateful.

I would also like to express my sincere appreciation to Kofi Odei Frimpong, whose meticulous editing and valuable insights have greatly enriched this book. Your expertise and dedication have not only enhanced the quality of this work but have also made the process a joyful experience.

Special thanks are due to Prophet Paul Kweku Nii Okai, whose spiritual guidance has been a beacon of light throughout this journey. Your wisdom and prayers have been a source of strength and inspiration.

Lastly, I wish to acknowledge all those who have contributed to this project, whether directly or indirectly. Your help, support, and encouragement have played a vital role in making this dream a reality. I am eternally thankful to each one of you for being a part of this wonderful journey.

May this book be a testament to what can be achieved with faith, love, and collaboration.

TABLE OF CONTENTS

CHAPTER ONE: THE TRANSFORMATIVE POWER OF RELATIONSHIPS - FROM BANKING TO INSURANCE

IN THE HEARTBEAT OF ACCRA'S HIGHSTREET

My professional odyssey commenced in the dynamic heart of Accra's Highstreet, a bustling hub brimming with ambition and tenacity. As a nascent banker, I was captivated by the city's relentless drive, its rhythm syncing with my own burgeoning aspirations. My early career was underpinned by a fervent belief: to network relentlessly, to be omnipresent at every pivotal gathering, aiming to carve a distinct niche for myself in the competitive world of banking.

NAVIGATING THE INTRIGUING MAZE OF POWER LUNCHES

Each day was a whirlwind of crisp business suits, sleek briefcases, and the tantalizing promise of influential connections at an unending series of networking events. Each handshake and exchange of business cards was imbued with potential, a possible gateway to professional advancement. I was a zealous participant in the high-stakes game of banking, constantly strategizing, with my car doubling as a mobile wardrobe, perpetually prepared for the next significant event on the horizon.

DEEP DIVE INTO THE BANKING EPOCH

In those initial banking years, my philosophy was anchored in a quantitative approach: the broader my network, the greater the chances of opening new doors. I prided myself on being the initiator of handshakes, a collector of business cards, seeing each as a valuable trophy. One vivid memory is an afternoon at a client's product launch, surrounded by potential allies yet facing the irony of a complete absence of business cards. That day, instead of a triumphal march, I was met with exhaustion and a creeping sense of disillusionment.

THE ELUSIVE NATURE OF NETWORKING IN BANKING

As time progressed, a void began to emerge beneath the surface of my bustling schedule. My interactions, though numerous, started to feel more like ephemeral business transactions rather than genuine, meaningful connections. Despite being surrounded by a multitude of faces, I felt increasingly adrift, yearning for something more profound and enduring in my professional relationships.

THE EPIPHANY THAT CHANGED EVERYTHING

It was amidst a particularly intense week, packed with back-to-back meetings, that a moment of clarity struck me. As I mechanically exchanged business cards in a crowded room, a fundamental question pierced my consciousness: Was this the career path I truly desired? Was this the life I had envisioned for myself? This introspection led to a pivotal realization: the essence of effective networking wasn't in the sheer volume of connections, but in their depth and quality.

THE JOURNEY TO INSURANCE - A NEW BEGINNING

This insight precipitated a major career shift: from the world of banking to the realm of insurance. This transition, while daunting, was immensely enlightening. In the insurance sector, I came to understand the intrinsic value of relationships. It was no longer about an impersonal collection of contacts; it was about fostering meaningful, long-lasting connections, aligning them with my personal and professional aspirations.

MASTERING THE ART OF STRATEGIC NETWORKING

I gradually recognized that the true foundation of my success lay in the depth and quality of my relationships. Each individual I connected with transformed from a mere acquaintance into a mentor, a supporter, an integral part of my professional evolution. These relationships evolved into my most valuable assets, enabling me to adeptly navigate the intricacies of a new industry and to grow exponentially as a professional.

THE PATH FORWARD

This chapter is not merely a recounting of the early stages of my career; it's a reflection on the transformative influence of relationships. As we delve deeper into this book, the narrative will reveal how strategic networking has been instrumental in shaping my journey across various fields – banking, insurance, entrepreneurial life, ministry, and family life. This is just the commencement of an enlightening expedition. As we turn the pages, let's embark on this journey together, exploring the profound impact of relationships in shaping a fulfilling and successful path.

CHAPTER TWO: BUILDING BRIDGES – THE ART OF STRATEGIC NETWORKING IN THE INSURANCE SECTOR

A NEW BEGINNING: EMBRACING THE UNKNOWN

This chapter of my career began not just with a change in industry but with a profound shift in mindset. The transition from banking to insurance was more than a mere job switch; it was a journey into uncharted waters, laden with uncertainties but brimming with potential.

1. The Thrill of Starting Anew

Leaving the banking sector, where I had built my career, felt like stepping off a familiar path into a dense forest of the unknown. There was a thrill in this new beginning, a sense of adventure. The world of insurance, with its unique challenges and dynamics, presented an opportunity to reinvent myself professionally, to learn, and to grow in ways I hadn't anticipated.

2. Embracing a Learner's Mindset

As I embarked on this new journey, I adopted a learner's mindset. I immersed myself in the insurance sector's intricacies, from understanding different insurance products to grasping the regulatory landscape. This humility to learn from scratch was both humbling and empowering, as it opened doors to new knowledge and perspectives.

3. The Challenge of Leaving Comfort Zones

Stepping into the insurance industry meant leaving behind the comfort and familiarity of banking. This transition was not just about learning new skills but also about unlearning old habits and assumptions. It challenged me to step out of my comfort zone, to question and reevaluate my approaches, and to be open to entirely new ways of thinking and working.

4. Building a New Professional Identity

This career shift was also an opportunity to build a new professional identity. In banking, I was known for specific skills and achievements. In insurance, I started anew, establishing myself based on new strengths, insights, and experiences. This process of rebuilding my professional identity was both challenging and exhilarating.

5. Navigating Initial Uncertainties

The initial phase was marked by uncertainties. There were moments of self-doubt and questions about whether I had made the right decision. However, these uncertainties also drove me to push harder, to prove to myself that I could thrive in this new environment.

6. The Excitement of New Opportunities

With every challenge came new opportunities. The insurance sector offered avenues to innovate, to engage with different types of clients, and to develop novel solutions to complex problems. Each day brought new learning experiences, each project a chance to apply my skills in fresh contexts.

7. The Support of Mentors and Peers

Transitioning to a new industry underscored the value of having mentors and supportive peers. Their guidance was instrumental in navigating the initial challenges. They provided insights, offered advice, and helped me build my network in the insurance world.

8. Celebrating Small Victories

Every small victory in this new field was a cause for celebration. Whether it was successfully closing my first insurance deal, receiving positive feedback from a client, or understanding a complex policy, these moments were not just achievements but milestones in my journey of adaptation and growth.

STRATEGIC NETWORKING: CRAFTING A NEW APPROACH

In the complex and interconnected world of insurance, I learned that successful networking goes beyond mere socializing; it requires a strategic, intentional approach. Here's how I refined my networking strategy to thrive in this new environment:

1. Identifying Key Influencers and Decision Makers

The first step was to identify the key players in the industry. This included not just top executives but also thought leaders, innovators, and rising stars. Understanding the landscape of influencers and decision-makers enabled me to focus my efforts on building relationships that were not only prestigious but also genuinely influential and insightful.

2. Quality Over Quantity

Gone were the days of collecting business cards without purpose. Each connection I sought was chosen for the value it could bring, both ways. This meant fewer, but more meaningful, relationships. It involved deeper conversations, more follow-ups, and a genuine interest in the people I connected with. This approach fostered trust and respect, laying the foundation for strong, lasting professional relationships.

3. Targeted Networking Events and Conferences

I became selective about the events I attended. Instead of trying to be everywhere, I chose events that aligned with my professional goals and areas of interest. This included specialized insurance conferences, seminars, and workshops. Attending these events with a clear objective in mind, whether it was to learn about a new trend or to meet a specific individual, made my networking efforts more effective.

4. Leveraging Mentorship and Advisory Relationships

Seeking mentors within the industry was a game-changer. These relationships provided invaluable insights and guidance. I sought individuals whose career paths or expertise aligned with my aspirations. In return, I offered my fresh perspective and enthusiasm, making these relationships mutually beneficial.

5. Building a Diverse Network

Diversity in networking meant connecting with professionals from various backgrounds, roles, and experience levels within the insurance sector. This diversity offered a wide array of perspectives and opportunities. It also meant stepping outside the insurance bubble at times, to bring in fresh ideas and approaches from other industries.

6. The Art of Listening and Learning

Strategic networking wasn't just about talking and self-promotion; it was equally about listening and learning. I made it a point to really listen during conversations, showing genuine interest in others' ideas, challenges, and successes. This not only helped in building rapport but also provided valuable learning opportunities.

7. Follow-Up and Relationship Maintenance

Effective networking doesn't end with the first meeting. I developed a system for following up and keeping in touch with my connections. This included regular check-ins, sharing relevant articles or information, and congratulating them on their achievements. These efforts kept the relationships alive and relevant.

8. Utilizing Digital Tools for Relationship Building

Incorporating digital tools into my networking strategy was crucial. LinkedIn, for instance, was not just a platform for connecting but also for engaging with contacts through likes, comments, and sharing content. This helped in maintaining visibility and relevance in my network.

9. Personalized Approach

I recognized that each connection was unique. I tailored my approach based on the individual's interests, career goals, and personality. This personalized approach made each interaction more meaningful and effective.

In essence, strategic networking in the insurance sector was about building a web of relationships that were carefully chosen, nurtured, and maintained. This deliberate and thoughtful approach not only enhanced my professional journey but also enriched my understanding and appreciation of the industry.

LEARNING FROM PAST MISTAKES: APPLYING HARD-EARNED LESSONS

Reflecting on my earlier career missteps, especially from my banking days, provided a fertile ground for growth in the insurance sector. Here's how I transformed those lessons into strategic advantages:

1. Valuing Depth over Superficial Connections

In my banking career, I often mistook the quantity of connections for quality. This approach led to many superficial relationships that lacked depth and value. In the insurance sector, I shifted my focus to building fewer but more meaningful relationships. This meant engaging in deeper conversations, understanding the challenges and aspirations of my connections, and fostering relationships based on mutual respect and shared interests.

2. Prioritizing Long-Term Goals over Short-Term Gains

Previously, I was often caught up in the immediate benefits of networking, missing the bigger picture. I learned to approach networking with a long-term perspective, focusing on how each relationship could evolve over time. This mindset shift helped me build a network that was not only robust but also aligned with my long-term career aspirations in the insurance industry.

3. Embracing Authenticity in Interactions

My past experiences taught me the importance of authenticity. In my banking days, I sometimes found myself adopting personas that didn't truly reflect who I was, in an effort to fit into certain circles. In insurance, I embraced my authentic self in every interaction. This authenticity fostered trust and genuine connections, which are invaluable in the industry.

4. Learning to Listen Actively

One of my earlier mistakes was focusing too much on speaking and not enough on listening. Active listening became a key component of my interactions. This not only helped me understand the needs and perspectives of others better but also allowed me to provide more meaningful contributions to conversations.

5. Efficient Time Management and Selectivity

In the past, I would attend almost any networking event, often leading to burnout and unproductive outcomes. I learned to be selective, choosing events and meetings that aligned with my goals and interests. This efficient use of time meant that I could dedicate more energy to each interaction, making them more productive and enjoyable.

6. Acknowledging and Learning from Failures

Previously, I tended to brush off failures rather than confronting and learning from them. In my new role, I embraced failures as learning opportunities. Whether it was a missed connection or an unsuccessful collaboration, each setback provided valuable insights that helped refine my approach to networking and professional growth.

7. Leveraging Technology Wisely

In the past, I underutilized the power of technology in networking. In the insurance sector, I learned to leverage digital tools and platforms not just for connecting but also for research, staying updated, and engaging with my network. This also included maintaining a well-curated online presence, which became an extension of my professional identity.

8. Avoiding Overcommitment

One of the biggest lessons from my banking days was the pitfalls of overcommitment. In my pursuit to make a mark in the insurance sector, I was mindful not to stretch myself too thin. I learned to say no when necessary, allowing me to commit fully to the engagements and relationships I chose to pursue.

These lessons from past mistakes were instrumental in shaping a more effective, fulfilling, and sustainable approach to networking and professional development in the insurance sector. Each misstep became a stepping stone to greater understanding and success.

THE POWER OF GENUINE CONNECTIONS: BEYOND BUSINESS CARDS

In the world of insurance, I discovered that the true essence of networking transcends the exchange of business cards and superficial interactions. It's about forging genuine connections that go beyond mere professional courtesies. Here's how I deepened these connections:

1. Building Relationships Based on Mutual Interests and Values

Rather than focusing solely on business potential, I sought to connect with individuals based on shared interests and values. This approach led to more engaging conversations and stronger bonds. Whether it was a shared passion for industry innovation, community service, or personal hobbies, finding common ground provided a solid foundation for lasting relationships.

2. The Art of Personal Engagement

I learned the importance of engaging with people on a personal level. Understanding their backgrounds, challenges, and aspirations allowed me to connect more deeply. This kind of engagement fostered a sense of trust and camaraderie, making business discussions more open and fruitful.

3. Cultivating Empathy and Understanding

Empathy became a key tool in my networking arsenal. By genuinely trying to understand the perspectives and challenges of others, I was able to build more meaningful and supportive relationships. This empathy also helped in providing tailored solutions and advice, further cementing these connections.

4. Offering Help Before Expecting It

I adopted a 'give first' approach. Offering assistance, sharing resources, or providing valuable introductions without immediate expectation of return not only helped others but also established my reputation as a supportive and valuable member of the network.

5. Celebrating Others' Successes

Celebrating the achievements of my connections was as important as sharing my own. Congratulating them on their successes, whether through a personal message, a public acknowledgment, or attending their celebratory events, helped strengthen our bond.

6. Nurturing Connections Over Time

Genuine connections require time and effort to nurture. I made sure to keep in touch, check in regularly, and stay updated with their professional journeys. This ongoing effort ensured that the connections remained strong and relevant.

7. Authenticity in Every Interaction

I ensured that authenticity was at the heart of every interaction. This meant being genuine in my conversations, staying true to my values, and being honest about my capabilities and intentions. People tend to resonate more with those who are authentic and transparent.

8. Shared Experiences and Stories

Sharing personal stories and experiences, and inviting others to share theirs, created a deeper level of understanding and connection. These stories often revealed common struggles, triumphs, and lessons, making our interactions richer and more relatable.

The power of genuine connections in the insurance sector cannot be overstated. It's about building relationships that are rooted in mutual respect, shared values, and personal engagement. These connections transcend the typical transactional nature of business networking, evolving into partnerships that are both professionally rewarding and personally fulfilling.

TOOLS AND TECHNIQUES: MODERNIZING NETWORKING

As I navigated the dynamic landscape of the insurance sector, I quickly realized that traditional networking methods were ripe for modernization. The transformation was not just about embracing new platforms but about rethinking the very essence of building and maintaining professional relationships.

1. Embracing Digital Platforms for Broader Reach

Social media, particularly LinkedIn, became an indispensable tool. It wasn't just a place to connect but a vibrant forum to showcase expertise, engage in meaningful discussions, and stay abreast of industry trends. I curated my online presence with care, ensuring it reflected my professional journey and insights. Sharing articles, participating in discussions, and offering commentary on industry news helped establish my voice in the insurance community.

2. Personal Branding: Crafting a Unique Professional Identity

Personal branding emerged as a key strategy. In a sea of professionals, it was crucial to stand out. I meticulously crafted my brand to reflect my values, expertise, and vision for the future. This went beyond just a professional headshot and a well-written bio; it was about consistently demonstrating my unique perspective and contributions to the field. My brand became my silent ambassador, opening doors and fostering connections.

3. Strategic Online Networking: Quality Over Quantity

I learned the art of strategic online networking. It wasn't about amassing contacts but about fostering meaningful relationships. I targeted individuals and groups that aligned with my professional interests and values. Engaging in smaller, focused online communities offered deeper, more meaningful interactions than larger but superficial networks.

4. Leveraging Webinars and Virtual Conferences

The digital age has revolutionized how we gather for learning and networking. Webinars and virtual conferences became crucial networking arenas. These platforms allowed me to connect with industry leaders and peers globally, transcending geographical limitations. Active participation in these events, through questions and follow-up discussions, often led to valuable connections and insights.

5. Podcasts and Blogs: Sharing and Gaining Knowledge

Creating and contributing to podcasts and blogs emerged as a powerful tool. By sharing my experiences and insights, I not only established my expertise but also engaged with a wider audience. Listening to and participating in others' podcasts and blogs provided continuous learning and networking opportunities.

6. The Art of Virtual Coffee Meetings

The concept of virtual coffee meetings became a staple in my networking toolkit. These informal, yet focused, online meet-ups allowed for personal connections in a time-efficient manner. They offered a space for candid conversations, knowledge exchange, and mutual support in a more relaxed setting.

7. Continuous Learning and Adaptation

I have come to recognize that networking techniques and tools are ever-evolving. Staying informed about the latest digital trends and adapting to new platforms and methods became an ongoing process. This continuous learning and adaptation ensured that my networking strategies remained effective and relevant.

THE JOURNEY CONTINUES: A COMMITMENT TO GROWTH

Reflecting on my journey in the insurance sector, I see a rich mosaic of relationships, strategies, mistakes, and triumphs. It's been a winding path, uniquely mine, carved out by deliberate choices and driven by a clear vision. My network has grown into something far more profound than a collection of contacts; it's a web of opportunities, friendships, and avenues for personal growth. The joy of making meaningful connections has added new dimensions to my professional life.

As I continue to navigate the ever-evolving landscape of the insurance world, my commitment to growth remains steadfast. It's a journey without a final destination, a continuous quest for improvement and connection.

In sharing these reflections, I invite you to see echoes of your own story in mine. May you find inspiration in my journey, learn from my missteps, and recognize the transformative power of strategic networking.

Let's turn the page together. A world of new possibilities and thrilling adventures awaits in the chapters to come.

CHAPTER THREE: GUIDING LIGHTS – MENTORSHIP, LEARNING, AND THE PATH TO MASTERY

THE JOURNEY OF GUIDANCE

In the complex world of insurance, I realized that support from others is crucial. Every successful person has a team of mentors and teachers who show them the way. When I started to learn more about this field, I understood that getting guidance was not just something nice to have; it was essential.

Navigating the Maze: Insurance, with its myriad of policies and regulations, is akin to navigating a labyrinth. Guidance becomes the thread that leads one through this maze, helping to avoid common pitfalls and uncover hidden opportunities.

The Power of Perspective: Mentors provide a unique vantage point, offering insights gained from years of experience. This perspective is invaluable in understanding complex scenarios and making informed decisions.

Building a Support Network: In insurance, relationships and networks are paramount. Mentors often serve as the gateway to broader professional networks, opening doors that might otherwise remain closed.

FINDING THE RIGHT MENTORS

A mentor is not just someone with experience; they are like a guiding star, full of wisdom and encouraging growth. But getting the right mentor is not just about luck; it requires effort.

Identifying Potential Mentors: Look for individuals who not only excel in their field but also resonate with your personal and professional values.
Fostering Relationships: Engage in industry events, online forums, and professional groups. Networking isn't just about meeting people; it's about connecting with the right people.

Mutual Benefit: Remember that mentorship is a two-way street. Consider what you can offer to your mentor, whether it's fresh perspectives, new ideas, or assistance with projects.

THE PATH OF CONTINUOUS LEARNING

Having a mentor helped me see that learning never stops. It's not just about knowing all about insurance; it's about always wanting to know more and being curious.

Embracing Curiosity: Stay inquisitive. Ask questions, seek out new information, and challenge your understanding.
Diversifying Learning Sources: Apart from traditional learning methods, explore webinars, podcasts, and industry publications.
Learning from Mistakes: View every mistake as a learning opportunity. Reflect on what went wrong and how it can be avoided in the future.

BUILDING A PERSONAL DEVELOPMENT PLAN

With a strong desire to learn, I knew I needed a plan. Growing without direction can be confusing and aimless. I needed a personal plan that set out my goals, how to reach them, and how to measure my progress.

Setting Clear Goals: Define what you want to achieve in your career. Break down these goals into actionable steps.

Flexibility and Adaptability: Be prepared to adjust your plan as circumstances change. The insurance industry is dynamic, and your plan should be too.

Measuring Progress: Establish metrics to track your development. Regularly review your achievements and areas for improvement.

MENTORSHIP AS A TWO-WAY STREET

As I became more experienced, I started to help others. Going from being mentored to being a mentor was a big and rewarding step. I started to pass on what I knew to those who wanted to learn.

Sharing Knowledge: Use your experience to guide newcomers. Share both your successes and your failures.

Empathetic Listening: Be an active listener. Understand the challenges your mentees face and provide tailored advice.

Continuous Learning: As a mentor, you also learn. Teaching others can provide new insights and deepen your own understanding.

A JOURNEY OF GROWTH AND DISCOVERY

The road to becoming an expert, learning, and helping others is a journey, not a place you reach. It's about always growing, learning new things, and helping others along the way.

Embrace Change: The insurance industry is ever-evolving. Stay open to new ideas and be ready to adapt.

Fostering a Community of Learners: Encourage a culture of learning within your network. Share resources, insights, and opportunities.

Reflecting on the Journey: Take time to reflect on your growth and the paths you've taken. Use these reflections to guide your future decisions.

As this part of the story ends, I want you to think about your own path. Look for guidance, keep learning, and be someone who helps others.

The adventure goes on. In the next part, we'll explore even more about the interesting world of insurance and the valuable lessons it has to teach.

CHAPTER FOUR: NAVIGATING STORMS – CHALLENGES, SETBACKS, AND LESSONS LEARNED

THE INEVITABILITY OF CHALLENGES

Unforeseen Obstacles as Catalysts for Growth

Life isn't just about smooth sailing; it's about learning how to navigate through storms. In the complex world of insurance, I've faced numerous challenges, each one a disguised teacher. These weren't mere roadblocks; they were the sculptors of my character, sharpening my skills and deepening my understanding. It's in the heart of these challenges that one truly discovers resilience and creativity.

Personal Anecdote: A Daunting Challenge

Reflecting on my journey, a particular challenge stands out – a regulatory hurdle that seemed insurmountable. It wasn't just about complying with new regulations; it was about redefining our approach to compliance itself. This daunting task taught me the value of adaptability and the importance of staying ahead of the curve.

FACING PROFESSIONAL SETBACKS

The Harsh Reality of Career Obstacles

No career is immune to setbacks. I've had my fair share, each bringing its blend of disappointment and self-doubt. Professional growth often sprouts from the soil of these setbacks, offering invaluable lessons in perseverance and humility.

Case Study: Overcoming a Failed Initiative

A particular project of mine – a groundbreaking policy design – failed despite meticulous planning and execution. This failure was a harsh teacher, revealing the unpredictability of market reception and the need for agile adaptation. It taught me the importance of contingency planning and the art of graceful failure.

LEARNING FROM MISTAKES

Embracing Errors as Learning Opportunities

Mistakes are often seen as career blunders, but I view them as vital learning opportunities. Each error has been a stepping stone to greater understanding and skill.

Real-Life Example: A Botched Negotiation

A negotiation that went sour despite thorough preparation taught me a crucial lesson: the human element in business dealings. It wasn't just about the figures; it was about understanding the client's underlying needs and fears. This experience reshaped my approach to negotiation, blending empathy with strategy.

OVERCOMING PERSONAL OBSTACLES

The Challenge of Maintaining Work-Life Harmony

In a demanding career, it's easy to lose sight of personal well-being. There was a time when work consumed me, blurring the lines between professional dedication and personal neglect. It took a toll on my relationships and health.

Journey Back to Balance

Acknowledging this imbalance was the first step. I learned to set boundaries, to find joy in hobbies, and to reconnect with loved ones. This journey back to balance was not just about personal well-being but about sustaining my professional effectiveness.

THE IMPORTANCE OF SELF-CARE

Self-Care: A Non-Negotiable Aspect of Success
In the relentless pursuit of career milestones, self-care often becomes an afterthought. However, neglecting it can lead to burnout and diminished effectiveness.

My Wake-Up Call: A Health Scare
A health scare was my wake-up call. It forced me to reevaluate my lifestyle choices. I embraced practices like mindfulness, regular exercise, and healthier eating habits. This transformation wasn't just about physical health; it was about nurturing mental and emotional resilience.

BUILDING A RESILIENT MINDSET

Cultivating Resilience: A Continuous Process

Resilience isn't inherent; it's cultivated through experiences. My professional journey has been a testament to developing this resilience, learning to view challenges not as setbacks but as opportunities for growth.

Strategies for Mental Strength

Building mental strength involved more than just enduring hardships; it required proactive strategies like meditation, seeking mentorship, and engaging in reflective practices. These tools have not only fortified my resilience but also enriched my life in profound ways.

COPING WITH STRESS AND UNCERTAINTY

Navigating the Unpredictable Waters of the Insurance Sector

The insurance sector, with its inherent uncertainties and pressures, has been a fertile ground for learning stress management and adaptability.

Personal Strategies for Coping

To cope, I've adopted various strategies like regular physical activity, maintaining a gratitude journal, and pursuing creative outlets. These practices have not only helped me manage stress but also brought a sense of balance and fulfilment.

THE BEAUTY OF THE STORM

Finding Meaning in Challenges

The true beauty of life's storms lies not in their chaos but in the lessons and transformations they bring. They're not just hurdles to overcome; they're opportunities to discover our true potential and forge a path of continuous growth.

A Journey of Continuous Discovery

As I turn the page to the next chapter, I do so with a sense of excitement and anticipation. The journey ahead is not just about overcoming obstacles; it's about embracing each experience as a chance for personal and professional enlightenment."

CHAPTER FIVE: CHARTING NEW WATERS – INNOVATION, ADAPTABILITY, AND STAYING AHEAD OF THE CURVE

THE EVER-CHANGING LANDSCAPE

Embracing the Flux: In the insurance industry, change is not just a challenge; it's an opportunity. By embracing the flux, companies can turn volatility into a competitive advantage. This involves staying alert to market shifts, leveraging data analytics for predictive insights, and being ready to pivot strategies in response to new developments.

Learning from the Past, Anticipating the Future: Successful companies analyze historical trends to anticipate future shifts. This proactive approach involves using data to identify patterns, predict customer needs, and stay ahead of regulatory changes. It's about learning from the past to navigate the future more effectively.

EMBRACING INNOVATION: THE IMPORTANT NEED FOR NEW IDEAS

Case Study - Pokuaa: The introduction of Pokuaa, an AI-powered WhatsApp chatbot for underwriting, initially met skepticism. However, by embracing this innovative technology, the company could streamline processes, improve customer engagement, and open up new avenues for data analysis and risk assessment.

Cultivating a Culture of Creativity: Innovation starts with culture. Companies that encourage creativity allow employees to think outside the box, challenge norms, and propose new ideas without fear of failure. This environment fosters a continuous flow of fresh ideas and innovative solutions.

LEADING AND JOINING IN NEW PROJECTS

Building and Nurturing Diverse Teams: Diversity in teams brings different perspectives and experiences, leading to more creative and comprehensive solutions. Effective leaders encourage collaboration among team members from varied backgrounds, fostering an environment where different ideas and approaches are valued.

Embracing Failure as a Teacher: Innovative projects often come with risks and the possibility of failure. Learning from these failures is crucial for growth. It involves analyzing what went wrong, adapting strategies, and building resilience to face future challenges.

ADAPTABILITY IN A CHANGING WORLD: DEALING WITH CHANGES IN THE BUSINESS

Case Study - Regulatory Adaptation: When faced with new regulatory challenges, a proactive approach involved conducting thorough analyses, engaging with stakeholders to understand impacts, and swiftly adapting operations to comply while maintaining efficiency.

Flexibility as a Strategic Advantage: Flexibility enables companies to respond quickly to market changes. This agility can be a significant advantage, allowing businesses to capitalize on opportunities more rapidly than competitors and adjust strategies in response to external pressures.

BUILDING A WAY TO CHANGE EASILY

Strategies for Effective Change Management: Successful change management involves clear communication, stakeholder engagement, and a structured approach to implementing changes. It's about guiding employees through transitions while maintaining productivity and morale.

Leveraging Change for Innovation: Change often brings new perspectives and opportunities for innovation. Companies that leverage change as an impetus for innovation can discover new markets, develop new products, and improve processes.

STAYING AHEAD: KEEPING AN EYE ON NEW TRENDS

Emerging Trends in the Insurance Industry: Staying ahead involves identifying and understanding emerging trends like digital transformation, customer-centric approaches, and sustainability. This foresight allows companies to align their strategies with future market demands.

The Role of Continuous Learning: In a rapidly evolving industry, continuous learning is crucial. This can involve regular training, attending industry conferences, and staying updated with latest research and publications.

PLANNING AND MAKING THE MOST OF THINGS

Case Study - Cyber Insurance: Identifying the rising demand for cyber insurance, a strategic plan was developed to not only enter this market but also to lead it. This involved researching market needs, developing tailored products, and establishing a strong brand presence in the new segment.

Strategic Alignment with Market Trends: This involves aligning the company's strategic goals with identified trends. It requires a deep understanding of how these trends impact the business and how to leverage them for growth.

WORKING TOGETHER AND LEARNING FROM OTHERS

Cross-Industry Collaborations: Collaborations with different industries can bring in new ideas and approaches. For instance, partnering with tech companies can introduce innovative tech solutions, while collaboration with academic institutions can provide access to cutting-edge research.

Networking and Relationship Building: Effective networking involves more than just making contacts; it's about building relationships that can provide mutual benefits, share knowledge, and open doors to new opportunities.

THE POWER OF TALKING TO PEOPLE AND MAKING FRIENDS

Case Study - Healthcare Collaboration: Collaborating with a healthcare technology company led to the creation of a personalized health insurance product. This venture combined expertise in insurance with innovative health tech solutions, resulting in a product that stood out in the market.

The Art of Networking: Successful networking is about engaging in meaningful conversations, exchanging ideas, and forming partnerships that can lead to collaborative projects and new business opportunities.

THE HARD AND GOOD THINGS ABOUT NEW IDEAS

Overcoming Resistance to Change: Introducing new ideas often faces resistance. Overcoming this requires effective communication, demonstrating the value and potential of new ideas, and engaging stakeholders in the process.

Learning from Success and Failure: Each project, whether successful or not, offers valuable lessons. Analyzing outcomes helps refine approaches, improve decision-making, and innovate more effectively in future projects.

CELEBRATING GOOD THINGS AND LEARNING FROM MISTAKES

Case Study - Learning from a Failed Product Launch: A product launch that didn't meet expectations provided an opportunity to learn. The analysis helped identify market misalignments, leading to improvements in market research and product development processes.

The Importance of Reflection and Analysis: Regular reflection and analysis of both successes and failures are crucial. This practice helps in understanding what works, what doesn't, and how to approach future projects more effectively.

THE NEVER-ENDING JOURNEY OF LEARNING

Cultivating a Mindset of Lifelong Learning: Embracing a philosophy of lifelong learning involves staying curious, seeking new knowledge, and being open to new ideas and approaches. It's about constantly evolving both personally and professionally.

The Excitement of Discovery: The journey of innovation and adaptability in the insurance industry is filled with discovery. It's a path that leads to continuous improvement, new opportunities, and the excitement of exploring uncharted territories.

CHAPTER SIX: THE PILLARS OF VIRTUE – ETHICS, INTEGRITY, AND SOCIAL RESPONSIBILITY

THE FOUNDATION OF TRUST: ANCHORING RELATIONSHIPS IN THE INSURANCE WORLD

Trust: The Invisible, Indispensable Bond - Trust is not just a concept; it is the invisible yet indispensable bond in the insurance industry. It acts as the unspoken promise, the underlying agreement in every interaction, the assurance that clients, partners, and the community can rely on us.

The Triad of Trust: Ethics, Integrity, and Social Responsibility - These are the triad that underpins trust. They are the steadfast anchors, the guiding principles that dictate how we conduct ourselves, make decisions, and impact society. They are the essence that sustains and nurtures the delicate fabric of trust.

UPHOLDING ETHICAL PRINCIPLES: GUIDING OUR JOURNEY IN INSURANCE

Core Values as Our Ethical Beacon - The core values of honesty, fairness, confidentiality, and respect are not just words; they are our ethical beacon. These values are deeply ingrained in every aspect of our business, shaping our interactions and forming the backbone of our products and services.

Living Our Principles in Action - These principles are brought to life in our daily operations. They influence our approach to client service, product development, and stakeholder engagement, ensuring an ethical approach in even the most routine tasks.

NAVIGATING ETHICAL DILEMMAS: STEERING THROUGH MORAL WATERS

Complexities of Ethical Decision-Making - Ethical dilemmas in insurance are complex and multifaceted. They require a deep understanding of our moral compass, challenging us to weigh the fine balance between business imperatives and ethical standards.

Case Study: Ethics vs. Profit - A real-life scenario where we faced a lucrative opportunity that clashed with our ethical guidelines. This situation tested our resolve, ultimately leading us to choose long-term ethical integrity over short-term financial gain, reinforcing our commitment to ethical standards.

INTEGRITY IN BUSINESS PRACTICES: THE CORE OF OUR PROFESSIONAL IDENTITY

Living Integrity Every Day - Integrity is more than a virtue; it's the essence of our professional identity. It permeates our communication, dealings, and decision-making, ensuring that we stay true to our word, our principles, and ourselves.

Case Study: Honesty in Negotiations - A detailed account of how integrity played a crucial role in a challenging negotiation, where transparency and honesty converted a potential conflict into a win-win situation, reinforcing the value of integrity in building strong business relationships.

BUILDING RELATIONSHIPS THROUGH INTEGRITY: CONSTRUCTING BRIDGES OF TRUST

Integrity as a Relationship Builder: Integrity is the cornerstone of building and maintaining relationships in our industry. It's a long-term investment that yields dividends in the form of credibility, loyalty, and a sterling reputation.

Examples of Relationship Building: Diverse instances where our commitment to integrity has fostered deeper connections with clients, creating bonds based on trust and respect, and ultimately enhancing our market standing and client loyalty.

THE ROLE OF SOCIAL RESPONSIBILITY: OUR COMMITMENT TO SOCIETY

Beyond Business: Our Social Fabric - Recognizing that the insurance industry is an integral part of society, our commitment to social responsibility goes beyond business. It's about making a positive impact, contributing to the greater good, and improving lives.

Community Engagement: More Than Corporate Responsibility - Our involvement in community projects, from financial education to environmental initiatives, demonstrates our commitment to social responsibility. These projects are not just corporate gestures; they are heartfelt endeavors that reflect our dedication to empowering and uplifting communities.

NAVIGATING ETHICAL CHALLENGES: A CONTINUOUS ETHICAL QUEST

Ethical Challenges: Navigating the Gray Areas - Ethical challenges in our field are complex, often presenting as shades of gray rather than clear black and white scenarios. They require a deep understanding of ethical principles, critical thinking, and the ability to empathize.

Case Study: Balancing Ethics with Legal and Moral Obligations - A complex case involving a claim dispute that presented both ethical and legal dilemmas. Our approach balanced regulatory compliance, contractual obligations, moral principles, and compassion, demonstrating the nuanced nature of ethical decision-making in our industry.

STRATEGIES FOR ETHICAL DECISION-MAKING: CRAFTING A COLLABORATIVE ETHICAL FRAMEWORK

Engaging Stakeholders in Ethical Decision-Making. Our approach to ethical decision-making involves engaging a diverse array of stakeholders. This collaborative approach ensures that multiple perspectives are considered, enriching our decision-making process.

Cultivating an Ethical Culture. Our commitment to ethics is reinforced through ongoing dialogues, workshops, and training sessions. These initiatives are vital in fostering an environment where ethical awareness and critical thinking are part of our organizational DNA.

LEARNING FROM MISTAKES: EMBRACING ERRORS AS OPPORTUNITIES FOR GROWTH

A Culture of Reflection and Learning: We view mistakes as opportunities for learning and growth. Our culture promotes ethical reflection, encouraging team members to learn from errors and continually enhance our ethical practices.

Learning Through Examples: We share instances where past mistakes have been transformed into valuable lessons, enhancing our understanding of ethical issues and improving our future responses.

THE IMPACT OF ETHICAL LEADERSHIP: INSPIRING INTEGRITY THROUGHOUT THE ORGANIZATION

Leadership as an Ethical Example: Leadership in our industry is about more than achieving business goals; it's about setting an example in ethical conduct. Our leaders embody the values of ethics and integrity, inspiring others to follow suit.

Case Study: Leadership in Action - An example where leadership played a critical role in upholding ethical standards, demonstrating that ethical values are paramount and non-negotiable in our organization.

THE RIPPLE EFFECT OF ETHICAL LEADERSHIP: EXTENDING INFLUENCE BEYOND THE TEAM

Mentoring Future Ethical Leaders: Our leaders actively mentor emerging professionals, emphasizing the importance of ethics and integrity and preparing them to be the next generation of ethical leaders in the insurance industry.

Broadening the Impact of Ethical Leadership: Our ethical leadership extends its influence beyond the immediate team, impacting employee behavior, client trust, organizational reputation, and the integrity of the insurance industry at large.

THE TIMELESS VALUES: ANCHORING IN AN EVER-CHANGING WORLD

Enduring Principles Amidst Change: Ethics, integrity, and social responsibility are not transient trends; they are timeless values that provide a steadfast anchor in the dynamic seas of business and societal change.

Embracing Your Ethical Compass: As we conclude this chapter, we invite readers to introspect and embrace their personal ethical values, committing to be beacons of integrity in their professional lives.

Forward to the Next Chapter: Looking ahead, the next chapter promises a continuation of our journey, rich with insights and reflections, as we remain anchored in our values, guided by our principles, and inspired by our responsibility to ourselves, our industry, and society.

CHAPTER SEVEN: LEADING THE FLEET – LEADERSHIP, TEAM BUILDING, AND ORGANIZATIONAL CULTURE

THE ESSENCE OF LEADERSHIP

Leadership in the insurance industry is a multifaceted role, requiring a balance of strategic insight, personal influence, empathy, and resilience. It's about guiding a team through uncertainty and change, setting a vision, and creating a culture where each member feels valued and empowered.

Visionary Leadership: It involves setting a clear, compelling direction for the future. A leader must articulate where the organization is heading and why, inspiring others to join in the journey. For instance, when introducing a new digital platform, I communicated its potential to revolutionize our client interactions, rallying the team around this shared goal.

Influence: A leader's influence is key in shaping the team's attitudes and behaviors. This can be seen in how a leader's endorsement of new policies can drive widespread adoption within the organization.

Empathy: Understanding and sharing the feelings of team members is crucial. It involves listening to their concerns, acknowledging their challenges, and providing support, thus fostering a culture of trust and openness.

Resilience: The ability to withstand and bounce back from setbacks is vital. In the volatile insurance market, resilience means staying focused on long-term goals despite short-term fluctuations.

LEADERSHIP STYLES AND PHILOSOPHIES

Understanding different leadership styles is essential for navigating the various situations encountered in the insurance industry. Each style offers unique advantages and can be adapted to different contexts.

Transactional Leadership: This style focuses on structure, rewards, and penalties to motivate employees. While effective in achieving short-term goals, it may not foster long-term loyalty or innovation.

Transformational Leadership: This style is about inspiring and motivating employees to exceed their own expectations. It's about being a role model and helping employees see the value and purpose in their work.

Servant Leadership: This approach emphasizes the leader's role as a servant first, prioritizing the needs of the team and organization. It's about leading by example and putting others' needs above one's own.

Adaptive Leadership: In the ever-changing insurance industry, being able to adapt and respond to new challenges is crucial.

This style involves encouraging flexibility and innovation among team members.

PERSONAL LEADERSHIP EVOLUTION

Over the years, my leadership style has evolved from being primarily authoritative to more empathetic and participative. This evolution was driven by the realization that true leadership is about empowering others to realize their full potential.

From Authoritative to Collaborative: Initially, I focused on directives and performance. However, over time, I shifted towards a collaborative approach, recognizing the value of team input and creativity.

Embracing Empathy and Authenticity: Learning to lead with heart and authenticity has been a transformative experience, enabling me to connect with my team on a deeper level and build stronger, more effective relationships.

BUILDING AND NURTURING TEAMS

Building a successful team in the insurance industry is about more than just assembling talent; it's about creating an environment where individuals can grow, collaborate, and achieve collective success.

Recruitment Based on Values and Cultural Fit: Hiring for cultural fit and shared values has been key in building a cohesive team that shares a common vision and works effectively together.

Fostering Growth through Continuous Learning: Investing in continuous learning and development has been crucial in keeping the team up-to-date with industry trends and enhancing their skills.

CULTIVATING COLLABORATION AND SYNERGY

Promoting a culture of collaboration and synergy is crucial for a high-performing team. This involves creating an environment where open communication, trust, and mutual support are the norm.

Ongoing Team Building: Regular team-building exercises and open forums help in building trust and fostering collaboration, leading to a more cohesive and effective team.

Celebrating Diversity: Embracing diversity within the team brings in different perspectives and ideas, leading to more innovative solutions.

CULTIVATING A POSITIVE ORGANIZATIONAL CULTURE

Creating a positive organizational culture is about more than just implementing policies; it's about living the values and beliefs that define the organization.

Living the Values: Ensuring that the organization's values are reflected in every action and decision helps in building a strong, unified culture.

Culture as a Shared Endeavor: Initiatives like the "Culture Champions" program help in making culture a collective responsibility, leading to increased engagement and a sense of ownership.

MANAGING CONFLICTS AND CHALLENGES

Effectively managing conflicts and challenges is a critical aspect of leadership. It involves understanding the underlying issues, facilitating dialogue, and finding constructive solutions.

Facilitating Dialogue in Conflicts: Encouraging open communication and empathy in conflict situations helps in finding mutually beneficial solutions and strengthening team bonds.

Turning Challenges into Opportunities: Viewing challenges as opportunities for growth and learning is key in maintaining a positive outlook and driving innovation.

MENTORSHIP AND EMPLOYEE DEVELOPMENT

Mentorship is a crucial aspect of leadership, providing guidance and support to help team members grow both professionally and personally.

Personalized Mentoring: Providing individualized mentorship tailored to the specific needs and aspirations of team members leads to more effective development.

Career Pathways and Continuous Learning: Offering clear career pathways and continuous learning opportunities keeps the team motivated and aligned with the organization's goals.

THE CONTINUING JOURNEY OF LEADERSHIP

Leadership is a continuous journey of growth, adaptation, and impact. It's about leading with vision, values, and heart, and constantly striving to inspire, empower, and make a difference.

This chapter invites readers to reflect on their own leadership journey, embracing the opportunities for growth and striving to be the leader who makes a meaningful difference in their organization. The next chapter awaits, promising new insights and opportunities for continued exploration in the dynamic world of insurance. Let's turn the page together, guided by our leadership and commitment to success.

CHAPTER EIGHT: SAILING DIGITAL SEAS – TECHNOLOGY, NETWORKING, AND BUILDING RELATIONSHIPS IN THE DIGITAL AGE

THE EVOLUTION OF DIGITAL NETWORKING IN THE INSURANCE INDUSTRY

The insurance industry, once rooted in traditional face-to-face interactions, has been transformed by the digital age. This transformation has redefined the parameters of customer engagement, collaboration, efficiency, and trust, establishing a new landscape filled with diverse opportunities and significant challenges.

GLOBAL OUTREACH AND OVERCOMING THE DIGITAL DIVIDE

Case Study: Small Insurance Firm's Digital Revolution

Situation: A small insurance firm, traditionally limited to a local clientele, faced the challenge of expanding its reach without the resources for large-scale physical expansion.

Action: The firm turned to social media platforms, primarily using targeted advertising and community engagement strategies to connect with potential clients in remote and underserved regions.

Result: This approach not only expanded the firm's client base geographically but also diversified its clientele. It showcased how digital tools could level the playing field for smaller firms, allowing them to compete with larger entities in the global market.

ADDRESSING DIGITAL DIVIDE

Challenge: Despite the advantages of digital networking, there existed a digital divide – a gap where certain groups lacked access to digital tools and the internet.

Solution: The firm addressed this by implementing accessible online platforms and initiating community outreach programs. These programs included webinars and online tutorials, designed to educate and onboard people unfamiliar with digital tools.

TRANSITIONING TO VIRTUAL SPACES

Embracing Platforms like LinkedIn:

Early Days: LinkedIn initially served as a digital resume and job search platform. Over time, it evolved into a vital networking tool for professionals across various industries, including insurance.

Impact: LinkedIn allowed the firm's professionals to connect with industry leaders, potential clients, and peers worldwide. It became a platform for sharing industry insights, discussing trends, and fostering professional growth, transcending traditional networking boundaries.

The Rise of Virtual Conferences:

Before Digital: Previously, conferences were largely in-person events, restricted by location, cost, and capacity.

Digital Transformation: The firm embraced virtual conferences, which eliminated many physical constraints. These online events enabled real-time collaborations with a global audience, offered cost-effective networking solutions, and allowed for a larger, more diverse participation, enriching the exchange of ideas and experiences.

REIMAGINING RELATIONSHIP-BUILDING IN THE DIGITAL CONTEXT

In the digital era, relationship-building transcends beyond conventional networking methods, embracing authenticity, engagement, and personalization.

STRATEGIES FOR DIGITAL ENGAGEMENT AND LONG-TERM RELATIONSHIPS:

Engagement through Email and Webinars:
Personalized Email Campaigns: The firm began using data-driven insights to tailor its email communications. By understanding client preferences and behaviors, the emails became more than just informational broadcasts; they became tools for engagement, offering relevant content and personalized interactions.

Interactive Webinars: Leveraging the power of webinars, the firm hosted online events focusing on industry trends, new products, and expert discussions. These webinars were designed not only to inform but also to foster a sense of community and interaction among participants, encouraging questions, discussions, and follow-up engagements.

Fostering Relationships via Virtual Meetups and Collaborations:

Virtual Coffee Chats: Recognizing the importance of informal interactions, the firm initiated virtual coffee chats. These were casual, scheduled video calls where professionals could connect on a more personal level, discussing industry experiences, challenges, and personal interests.

Online Collaborative Projects: The firm also encouraged collaboration on digital platforms. It involved clients and partners in collaborative projects, using tools like shared digital workspaces and cloud-based project management software. This approach not only fostered a sense of partnership but also allowed for continuous, real-time collaboration, enhancing the depth and quality of professional relationships.

In this chapter, we have explored the multifaceted transformation of networking in the digital age within the insurance industry, highlighting how digital tools and platforms have opened new horizons for global outreach, personalized engagement, and strengthened relationships. The journey from traditional methods to embracing the digital landscape illustrates a significant shift in strategic networking, underscoring the importance of adaptability and innovation in the ever-evolving digital world.

CHAPTER NINE: BRIDGING GLOBAL SHORES – INTERNATIONAL NETWORKING AND CULTURAL INTELLIGENCE

THE GLOBAL LANDSCAPE OF NETWORKING

In today's world, networking transcends local and national boundaries, creating a vibrant and interconnected global business ecosystem. Consider the dynamic interplay between various sectors like insurance, technology, and manufacturing. This is not merely about exchanging business cards; it's about sharing perspectives, innovations, and strategies.

Global Interconnectivity and Transcending Geographical Limitations: Take the insurance industry, for example. A policy developed in New York might be underwritten in London and cover risks in Tokyo. Similarly, a software developer in Bangalore could collaborate effortlessly with a team in Silicon Valley. These examples illustrate how the digital era has dissolved geographical barriers, enabling an unprecedented flow of ideas and opportunities.

UNDERSTANDING CULTURAL DIVERSITY IN NETWORKING

Networking across the globe requires a deep understanding of and respect for cultural diversity. Each culture presents its distinct set of values, traditions, and business practices, enriching the tapestry of global commerce.

Embracing Cultural Nuances and Case Studies: In Japan, the ritual of exchanging 'Meishi' (business cards) with both hands signifies respect and acknowledgement. During my business dealings in China, I learned the importance of 'Guanxi' or relationship-building. Here, business is often preceded by social interactions, emphasizing the importance of personal bonds over immediate transactions.

NON-VERBAL COMMUNICATION

Non-verbal cues are as diverse as the cultures they originate from. They play a crucial role in communication and can significantly impact business relations.

Cultural Interpretation of Gestures and Personal Experiences: For instance, while a bow in Japan signifies respect, a firm handshake is preferred in the U.S. In Brazil, a thumbs-up is a positive gesture, but in some cultures, it could be misinterpreted. During my time in the Middle East, I observed the importance of appropriate eye contact and being mindful of personal space, which varied vastly from Western norms.

BUILDING RELATIONSHIPS ACROSS CULTURES

Creating and maintaining cross-cultural relationships is a journey that demands continuous learning, understanding, and adjustment.

Respecting Hierarchies, Time, and Long-term Commitments: In South Korea, acknowledging and respecting hierarchical structures is vital in business interactions. Similarly, in Germany, punctuality is not just appreciated but expected. Understanding these nuances is crucial for building lasting relationships. In countries like Italy, business dealings are often viewed through a familial lens, emphasizing long-term commitments and loyalty.

THE DIGITAL BRIDGE OF CONNECTION

The advent of digital platforms has revolutionized how we network internationally, turning the world into a small, interconnected village.

Leveraging social media for Global Reach: Platforms like LinkedIn and Twitter have emerged as powerful tools for global networking. They allow professionals to connect, share ideas, and foster relationships beyond physical boundaries. For example, a simple tweet could lead to a meaningful business collaboration across continents, demonstrating the transformative power of digital networking.

COLLABORATION TOOLS

Technology has significantly reduced the impact of physical distance in business, enabling real-time collaboration across the globe.

Virtual Collaboration and Global Team Dynamics: Tools like Zoom and Microsoft Teams have made it possible to brainstorm, discuss, and innovate with colleagues from different parts of the world as if they were in the same room. This virtual collaboration brings together a richness of perspectives and expertise, enhancing creativity and problem-solving.

STRATEGIES FOR EFFECTIVE INTERNATIONAL NETWORKING

Navigating the complexities of international networking requires strategic planning, cultural understanding, and thorough preparation.

Understanding Business Norms and Consulting Experts: Effective networking involves not only researching different cultural practices but also seeking insights from local experts. This approach helps in appreciating the subtleties of international business etiquette and avoiding cultural missteps.

LANGUAGE AND COMMUNICATION

In the realm of international networking, language serves as both a bridge and a barrier. It is essential for effective communication and relationship-building.

Investing in Language Skills and Utilizing Translation Tools: While mastering every language is impractical, learning key phrases and greetings in different languages demonstrates respect and effort. Additionally, the use of translation tools can aid in overcoming language barriers, making interactions more accessible and meaningful.

GLOBAL ALLIANCES AND PARTNERSHIPS

Forming global alliances involves aligning visions, strategies, and cultures, which can be both challenging and rewarding.

Navigating Negotiations and Building Shared Visions: Understanding the nuances of negotiations in different cultures is crucial. For example, in Japan, indirect communication is preferred, requiring a different approach than in more direct cultures.

Establishing a shared vision and values is fundamental in creating sustainable and impactful partnerships.

THE GLOBAL ORCHESTRA OF NETWORKING

International networking can be likened to conducting an orchestra where each participant plays a unique but harmonious part.

Harmonizing Cultural Differences: In this global orchestra, each culture contributes its unique melody. The conductor's role is to harmonize these diverse notes, creating a symphony that resonates across borders. This metaphor beautifully encapsulates the essence of global networking, underscoring the importance of understanding, respect, and collaboration.

International networking is a dynamic and enriching journey that requires an ever-evolving set of skills and perspectives. It's about embracing the world's diversity with curiosity and empathy, recognizing that every connection brings a new horizon, a fresh perspective, and a deeper understanding. This journey is not just about building a network; it's about weaving a rich tapestry of relationships that spans the globe.

CHAPTER TEN: THE FUTURE CANVAS – VISION, ADAPTATION, AND THE ENDLESS JOURNEY OF NETWORKING

THE ROAD TRAVELLED AND THE PATH AHEAD

The journey of networking is akin to an intricate dance, a series of steps leading us through a myriad of experiences and growth. Each interaction, each connection, is like a brushstroke on the canvas of our professional lives, creating a picture rich with lessons, insights, and transformations. As we look to the future, a landscape of opportunities, challenges, and uncertainties emerges, beckoning us to explore and adapt.

Example: Consider the story of Sarah, a marketing professional. In her early career, Sarah attended numerous networking events, collecting business cards and forging connections. Over time, these connections evolved into a robust professional network, offering opportunities and insights that shaped her career trajectory.

FROM HANDSHAKES TO DIGITAL CONNECTIONS

The shift from traditional, in-person networking to digital connections reflects not just a change in method, but also a transformation in our professional ethos. We recall the tangible, personal nature of handshakes, the energy of face-to-face conversations at industry events. Now, digital platforms like LinkedIn and virtual conferences have bridged physical distances, but the essence of human connection persists.

Example: When David transitioned from attending local business meetups to engaging in online webinars and LinkedIn discussions, he noticed a shift in his networking approach. While the medium changed, his objective of building meaningful relationships remained constant.

THE CONSTANT: HUMAN CONNECTIONS IN A CHANGING LANDSCAPE

No matter how much the landscape changes, the heart of networking remains rooted in human connections. Technology evolves, trends shift, but the pursuit of empathy, shared goals, and meaningful relationships endures. This constancy reminds us that our humanity transcends the tools and methods we use.

Example: Emily, a tech entrepreneur, uses various social media platforms to connect with peers and mentors. Despite the digital medium, her focus on empathy and mutual support remains a cornerstone of her networking strategy.

THE FUTURE OF NETWORKING

The integration of AI and data analytics into networking heralds a new era of personalized connection. Envision a world where algorithms suggest potential collaborators or mentors aligned with your career goals and interests. Networking platforms could become adept at understanding our unique networking needs, enhancing the impact and relevance of each connection.

Example: Imagine a platform that analyzes John's professional interests and career trajectory, suggesting a connection with Alex, an expert in a field John is keen to explore. This AI-driven approach could lead to more meaningful and strategic networking opportunities.

VIRTUAL AND AUGMENTED REALITY: THE NEXT FRONTIER

The incorporation of VR and AR into networking could revolutionize the way we interact virtually. Imagine attending immersive conferences where participants, despite being miles apart, feel like they're in the same room, engaging in lifelike conversations and collaborations. This could dismantle geographical barriers, offering experiences that closely mimic physical interactions.

Example: A virtual reality conference where Lisa, a designer in New York, and Akira, a developer in Tokyo, collaborate as if they were in the same room, discussing and visualizing projects in real-time.

ETHICAL CONSIDERATIONS: THE PILLARS OF TRUST

In a digital age, trust, privacy, and ethics become increasingly significant. Establishing trust in digital networks requires a steadfast commitment to ethical principles, transparency, and privacy protection. The future of networking should be underpinned by these values, ensuring integrity and respect in all interactions.

Example: A networking platform that prioritizes user consent and transparency in data usage, building trust among its users and ensuring that their privacy is respected.

EMBRACING CHANGE

The future is an unwritten canvas, and our ability to adapt is the brush we wield. Adaptability involves not just reacting to change but anticipating and embracing it, turning it into a growth opportunity.

Example: Michael, a business owner, stays abreast of market trends and technological advancements, ensuring his business strategies and networking approaches remain relevant and effective.

THE ENDLESS JOURNEY

Networking is an art without a final stroke; it's an ongoing exploration, an evolving dance. The relationships we build, the connections we forge, and the values we uphold are part of a continuous narrative, a collective story that we write together.

Example: As Ana's career progresses, she continually nurtures her existing connections while exploring new ones, understanding that networking is a lifelong journey.

THE SYMPHONY OF STRATEGIC NETWORKING

Strategic networking is akin to a symphony composed of diverse notes and harmonious melodies. Mastery in this art is a journey, an ongoing process of learning, adapting, and connecting.

As we conclude this book, let's carry forward the wisdom, insights, and connections we've gleaned, recognizing that our journey in the art of networking is ever-ongoing, filled with promise, potential, and the unbreakable power of human relationships.

REVIEW

In this book, you'll learn that networking isn't about knowing everyone and being everywhere as some people assume. Rather, it's about connecting with the right people, at the right time, in the right place. Networking must not be perceived as a numbers game, but as a relationship game.

As we navigate through our professional lives, the value of human connections becomes increasingly apparent. This book will help you to relate to the right tools that will help propel your career and life forward.

As a professional marketer and a pastor who deals with people on daily basis, I see this book as a very useful tool for anybody who desires to be a high flier. I strongly recommend this book.

Pastor Jerry Panou (Founder/ President, Accra Bible Seminary, Founder/ Head Pastor, Disciple Nations Church, Director, Word Finance Investment)

Note